TRANSITIONING FROM CHEMICAL LIVING TO A NATURAL LIFESTYLE

Erika G. Prentovitch

BALBOA.PRESS

A DIVISION OF HAY HOUSE

Balboa Press books may be ordered through booksellers or by contacting:

Balboa Press
A Division of Hay House
1663 Liberty Drive
Bloomington, IN 47403
www.balboapress.com
844-682-1282

Print information available on the last page.

ISBN: 978-1-9822-7789-5 (sc)
ISBN: 978-1-9822-7790-1 (e)

Balboa Press rev. date: 12/15/2021

CONTENTS

ACKNOWLEDGEMENTS

There are many I have to be grateful to for my path into the wild and guidance in the kitchen.

I thank my parents most of all for instilling in me a thirst for knowledge and a driving ambition to always dig for the true facts.

My father started me on this path at an early age, guiding me to edibles in the forest.

The women in my family saw to my domestic training, teaching me to properly clean and prepare our wild treasures into salves, infusions, tinctures, preserves and daily food.

As I aged, new teachers from different cultures came into my natural journey. I was blessed with gifts of knowledge from Native and European elders. These people generously provided me with insight to how things were done in places such as Scotland, Austria, Germany, Italy, Hungary, Poland, Czechoslovakia, Croatia, Holland and Scandinavian countries.

My appreciation also goes to numerous authors, who wrote invaluable field guides. I took every opportunity to read them, increasing my foraging knowledge.

I have written this book and my heart overflows with joy for all the kindness and support my family, friends and clients have shown me.

They never gave up on me, even when my self-esteem slipped. I was always given encouragement to keep moving forward.

My heartfelt Thanks & Blessings
Erika

INTRODUCTION

Hello and Welcome to a beneficial and a wise life choice!

You may not realize it yet, but you are about to cross over the threshold to a new world of existence.

This may sound dramatic and the experience most certainly is!

It's not just a change in eating habits or cleaning solutions, but so much more.

You shall find that by incorporating wild plants and herbs into your daily diet and routine, creates a monumental change that benefits your whole way of living.

Your level of healing energy shall alleviate muscle or pain issues you had…. that's right, Had! They shall gradually disappear. Other illnesses or diseases should diminish or cease to exist altogether. Our nature's bounty is that powerful. We have just lost touch with our ancient wisdom, faith and simple belief in our planet giving us all that we require.

Actually, some of these plants are literally right outside our door.

You may walk by them each day without notice. Once you do learn about these, so-called "Weeds" that are beneficial to you personally, you won't walk on your path, lawn or through any forest the same way again.

It shall awaken a new found or ancestral awareness of the wonders around you and what a gift our planet really is. One of the reasons I'm writing this book, to open eyes that have become clouded. There are many ways this shall change your entire household forever.

Once your clothes are washed with natural chemical free soaps, you'll notice mood shifts, better skin health, heightened respiratory function and most likely a better night's sleep. This also applies to the cleaning of your home and carries into lawn and garden care as well. Let's also not forget our fur baby family member's good health too.

Many people have seen my lifestyle ways and enjoyed products I've created from wild crafted plants for their specific needs. They always say the same thing, "I wish I could do that! or I'd love to be able to live as you do!" My reply is always the same, "You can, the only one stopping you… Is You!"

It's never a favoured answer, but true nevertheless.
This is yet another reason for this book, to help those that really would like this lifestyle but don't know where to begin. I'm here to make it simple and guide you to natural success!

So…. Why me? Well let me tell you a little about my background.

I come from a multicultural, European family tree. My parents were Austrian, a Croatian Oma, an Aunt from Czechoslovakia and many more relatives from Germany. These men and women grew up in small villages and some in the mountains where simple life meant survival. To my benefit, I was taught their knowledge from toddler on up to when I had children of my own.

I am now 59, my four sons are grown with lives of their own and I am blessed with two grandchildren. My motherhood began when I was 21 years of age and for the last forty years I have put my knowledge of the old ways to daily practical use.

I was a single mother for a large portion of that time while my boys were young and into their teens, which helped my financial state immensely.

Although my knowledge back then was limited to cuts, burns, fevers, colds, stomach aches and the like. It wasn't until my health took a turn for the worse that I really advanced in my natural skills.

I developed kidney issues, severe migraines, muscle issues, bladder infections plus other ailments such as blood poisoning and gum abscesses. I increased my studies to read all I could and finding people "in the know", my elder tribe. The elders I was led to were of many cultures as I mentioned in the acknowledgements.

These herbalists and elder healers gave me the ability to expand my knowledge to heal all of my body's issues.

To this day I am pharmaceutically drug free for twenty years, not even a Tylenol or Advil. There are still days I get a headache from pressure change, but I can get rid of it myself within about twenty minutes most times or less. I never concern myself with coming into contact with illness due to the herbs I keep flowing through my body on a daily basis as a preventative measure. Whatever life seems to place on my path, Mother Earth has the way for me to overcome that challenge. It is my fondest wish to resurrect this ancient knowledge to as many as I can, bringing happiness and harmony Mind, Body & Spirit. For if the body is strong and in good health, the mind cannot help but be in a highly aware and clear state, which puts the Spirit in a happy and harmonious element. When this combination is achieved, the belief and faith in each of us is in a giving capacity where it is shared.

This is the world I wish for! A world of each living being honouring one another.

May you enjoy your journey through this book and perhaps on to your....

Transitioning From Chemical Living To A Natural Lifestyle.

MEDICAL DISCLAIMER

Within these pages you shall be given advice from my research, experiments and "My" experiences. I am not a doctor or even a licensed herbalist and make no such claims. I encourage you to do your due diligence and research on your own too. What I am is a woman who chose to follow her ancestral guidance to living a simple life of nature. That I have done so and lived reasonably well to the age of 59, say's I made the right choices.... For Me!

This life may not be for everyone. A good measure of faith and belief goes along with it too. I still urge you to have connections with a Naturopath of good repute. Make sure to research this person you decide to trust with your health and that of your family. Just like hiring a contractor, there are good and then...not so much. In this case, it's not just about doing the job over right. You may not get another chance!

WHAT YOU NEED
TO KNOW FIRST

Anything and everything can be achieved, if you desire it! I shall try to make this as simple as possible but it takes genuine effort on your part. Don't just wish for this lifestyle, make it happen. The difference between desiring and just wishing, is achieving your goal or putting it on the shelf to get around to it as time continues to pass by. Make your choice count to benefit your good health.

The very first step is to invest in a good plant identification field guide book. Something small enough to carry in your foraging bag and have handy when you go out.

It is very important to know your plants, at least the specific one you are looking for. Do not assume anything!

For instance, that you can use the entire plant. Some plants it's acceptable to use the flower or the leaves but not the roots or vice versa.

This is especially the case when foraging for mushrooms and fungus. There are many plants that seem common and harmless, but taken in too high of quantities or for too long, can be disastrous. There are also other facts to take into consideration, for example if the recipient is a child, pregnant woman or perhaps has allergies.

It is a common condition for many these days to have allergic reactions to the Daisy family. Yet there are several wonderful plants out there that are related to this family, such as Goldenrod.
You may think I am trying to dissuade you from foraging, I am not. However, I am stressing the extreme importance of research, study and a huge portion of common sense.

I have used myself as a guinea pig for many things over the years, but I did not just jump in and start eating or using whatever plant I found. I looked into what I had found and studied the facts, searching in many places. I also did not rely upon just one source and most definitely not just the internet. My rule of thumb was this…. If I found corresponding facts from three or four reputable sources, then I entered that fact in my plant journal.

Again, I make the point of study and research, not to overwhelm but to accentuate the importance. Like any project undertaken, it is easier when broken down into steps.

The next step is to assess your reason for making this life change. This shall help you with a starting point and determine if you would like to make your own cleaners, personal products or begin to change to a healthier dietary source.

It could be you are looking to resolve a medical issue that has not gone well according to traditional pharmaceutical medicines. Whatever the case, when you have a starting point you can search out one or two plants that will work for your needs. Myself, in my early years I didn't do things quite so organized or with finesse. No, I started making little crib notes about every plant I saw on scraps of paper and was left with a stacked mess that was much harder to sort through when I did have need of them. I'm trying to save you the stress of my stresses. For example, let's say you decide to boost your immune system and your research leads you to Dandelions (one of my all-time favorites, you just can't mess up with Dandelions!)

The very first thing on your list of preparation, is to start a foraging journal. I can't put enough emphasis on the importance of this step!

Think like a scientist, you experiment, record your findings, experience failures, and experiment again and again…. repeating this process. You shall most definitely be adding after each experiment. It's a sure way for you to remember correctly your steps, quantities used and the end results. Discovering plants should also not be daunting, this is just another learning experience, so have fun.

In today's society, we have many conveniences to educate ourselves. There are plant identification apps to access with the snap of a picture. These are not failsafe or completely reliable and should not be your main source of identification, but it is sometimes a starting point for a name or family group. Having a name and your field guide with you gives you a good advantage, allowing you the ability to compare notes of the app and from within your book. If still unsure, leave it alone till you can find more accurate information. There is a good reason for the adage, "Better safe than sorry." Also having a person or elder in the "know", is very beneficial, don't discount some old fashioned ways of educating yourself.

Many times that information is priceless, as it's been handed down verbally from generation to generation. Our great great ancestors were not as ignorant as we may think of them. I would definitely say that "Researching" your plants are the most important part of "Natural Living". Further still, more than most companies do not have your best interests at heart, you have to be in the know and do your due diligence. The benefits of this are extremely self-satisfying.

When we think about helping our own day to day health, we have lost our faith to believe we can retain good health each and every day. There are herbs and wild plants that can keep us from ever getting sick and enjoying the quality of life we are meant to. Unfortunately to today's standards we have ads and fads telling us what to eat, what to put on and in our bodies, what to clean our homes and clothes with, etc., etc., etc.

Plus, the saddest fact, when we're told or made to believe we are eating nutritiously and healthy…. They Lie to us!!!

Food industries, Pharmaceutical companies become "Large" by concerning themselves with their profit margins, not your good health. Relying on your own personal knowledge will get you much farther along the path of "Good Health" …. If you're willing to put in the effort.

Another very important fact that is paramount on the road to good health and clean living, is one word…. "Quality"! What does this mean? Not nearly enough importance is placed on good quality products. Someone may choose organic vegetables, then purchase non organic meat from the grocery shelves coming from some large organization that have questionable methods to how the animals are fed and treated. Then there are hygiene products, such as deodorants, shampoo's and conditioner or household cleaners, soaps, dish and laundry detergents. All labeled, "Green Clean", yet most still contain SLS (Sodium Lauryl Sulfate), which can cause heart attacks, internal organ damage and cognitive damage. Buying some good quality products and some poor quality products does not serve your best interests. It has to be a complete circle. Prioritize where the higher damage is coming from and replace that product. It's one thing to replace a few products in your pantry at a time, but quite another to keep going back and forth from good to poor choices.

We are back to research, know what you are ingesting and surrounding yourself with. In other words, if you are going to buy anything…. Source your products.

This is an added benefit of foraging or growing your own supplies. However, this too comes with the task of sourcing your plants.

Here are a few facts to know when collecting or buying your plants or products.

ORGANIC, means the farmer is licensed and required to follow guidelines…. but they are still allowed to use a lower percentage of pesticides than a non-organic farmer.

NO-CHEMICAL, means exactly that, they are growing completely natural, without the use of pesticides. This is more labour intensive so prices shall most likely be higher.

FORAGED, means you or whomever you buy from has collected them from the wild. Something to pay attention to here, is know where the plant was taken from. For instance, if it was collected from a roadside ditch.... Does the township spray the ditches? Also, they may mow the roadside first and then spray. A good way to determine this is to look at the mowed grass and bushes nearby, if they are turning brown and drying up, it's a good bet they have been poisoned. Another tip is if you are foraging next to a farmer's field that may be sprayed with pesticides. When it rains that pesticide leeches and runs into the soil farther away too and contaminates all that grows or lives there.

ANIMAL HUSBANDRY, means how an animal is being cared for. Does the animal receive organic feed? Does it get vaccinated? Is the water supply received, chlorinated, have antibiotics added or worse, is there fluoride in the water (a nasty subterfuge)?

All these things require your knowledge to bring you the best quality food you can claim for good health, nutrition and lifestyle. What you ingest, put on your skin, hair and surround yourself with is the most important actions you can take to achieve your highest good in all ways! Also, do not be fooled by "No Scent" products, these too are filled with undetected toxins.

I'm often told cost plays an important role for many and it certainly does. I live on a less expensive budget, since I'm spending my money on the things I wish to rather than toxic products for my necessities. There are great savings to be had when Mother Nature offers to foot most of the bill. Despite the fact we all budget one way or another, there are many significant benefits to be had.

Choosing a natural lifestyle favorably affects your entire existence and it's operating function. When your body is in a dynamic working state, your mind is sharper, your sleep patterns correct themselves, your moods and emotions then function on a stress free, happier avenue. Which now affects how you conduct yourself with others and in society. It also enriches your body enough to evaluate your life path expectancy. Now multiply this throughout your entire family and household…. Doesn't this now look like a happy home life!

Go another large step and imagine if your neighbors and the entire town began to put this lifestyle in place. Are you seeing a better world, a better Earth? If each person, one by one begins to take a step towards self-betterment, the collective shall follow.

You may say a dream…. I say a Vision! :))

PREPARING YOUR SPACE

Organizing yourself, tools and space shall make the transition run so much smoother. I can still remember when I first started. I was so excited after reading my first book, seeing pictures of plants I already knew and passed by on walks all the time. I was thrilled to learn what the book said they could do, and I could use it as food. One was good for pain and another for skin rashes. Others could be used in salads, soups and stews…. I was Hooked!!!

I had no idea just how hook, line and sinker I really was hooked. This is where things got dicey. Out the door I went, my trusty Golden Retriever (Rascal) by my side, just as excited as I was to be heading into the forest. I took a grocery bag and a utility knife, and I was gone.

I lived in the country so there was a forest we always walked through. As we entered the field I looked at the plants surrounding me, realizing many looked the same without the flowers to tell them apart. Where was my field guide book to confirm my finds? Why back in the house, on the kitchen table of course. I didn't want to go back empty handed, I'm much too stubborn for that. So I thought, well I certainly know a Dandelion and what Thistles look like.

I found a patch of Dandelions and took out my utility knife to get roots. Ha Ha Ha!!!

My knife went into the dirt beside the stem and leaves.... And Snap!!! I hit a rock!

My knife blade had broken! With a big sigh I thought, " Where there's a will, there's a way" (Bless my Mom's old saying ringing in my head). Altered plan, I picked Dandelion leaves and flowers by hand. Well! Now my hands were all sticky from the Dandelion milk! Yes! It was a test of patience, will and I planned to win it.

Next was the Thistle. I wanted the leaves, stock and the root. No gloves (back at the house)! No knife, and my only bag was almost full with Dandelions.

Okay, maybe I could carefully pick a few leaves. Ouch! Nope! Not today, I'm not that stubborn.... or foolish. Rascal watched me the whole time, hahaha. What must he have thought of his mistress this day :)

We arrived home and I eyed my book on the table, the extra bags and my garden gloves with contempt, but definitely counted it a valuable lesson learned. Then I heard my Dad's voice in my head, "A good worker never blames their tools". Although, I certainly wasn't feeling it, and it just kept getting better from there. I realized I had nothing set up for drying. With very limited space in my home, I wasn't prepared for the next step.

I transferred the Dandelions to a paper bag so they wouldn't mold. I had plans to make bread with the flowers, back when I still ate bread. Next mistake (lesson), I wasn't able to make the bread the following day and thought, no harm, they're in a paper bag. Nope! I had wishes galore I could make with all the Dandelion fluff that was waiting for me in that paper bag.

This is why you organize, prepare and…. Study!!! :)))

So, what do you actually need….

To start with, acquire a good identification field guide book for your area and study plants that meet your needs. Begin with one or two at a time so that you are not overwhelmed.

Here are my suggestions, you may add or subtract from this list as you become more involved, but it's a starting point.

A Journal - I suggest a three ringed binder, so you can add pages and keep them alphabetically ordered for easy future reference. Leave yourself a full page for each plant, you shall be continually adding to it. Write the name of the plant in the top right hand corner of the page, so you can just flip through the top corner to find what specific plant you are looking for. A tip for quick and easy access. It's also advisable to document the Latin name as well, some plant families are very similar when researching (e.g... the Daisy clan).

Then leave a space about 3x4 inches under the name to do a simple little sketch. Oh, I can already hear the, "but I can't draw". This doesn't have to be perfect, just an allowance of recognition for you. Add any written identification notes for yourself (e.g.... picked by gate at Tailor's Lane). This will help you remember where it grows naturally, if you have to go back for more.

Now start recording useful information about the plant using headings (e.g..... Uses, Edible parts, Toxicity or Warnings, etc...) and I recommend writing in double space format, so you can add little notes at a later date if you wish to. If you can find vitamin and mineral content information, that is invaluable. If you are a Spiritual practitioner, you can use a separate sheet to record those benefits as well. I personally keep a third sheet for favored recipes too.

Always remember two phrases when researching…" Benefits of….and Side effects of", this shall give you in depth information. Take nothing for granted and assume nothing! Also take into consideration if you are creating a remedy…Are you or the recipient taking any other medication that may conflict or are there any allergies involved. If you are not sure, stay away from it till you have the correct information.

Foraging Bag or Basket - I prefer to carry a heavy canvas over the shoulder bag that has all my tools, extra bags, etc… in it and I keep it in my car for those unexpected finds.

These are the tools in my bag….

Scissors - Most times scissors are the perfect cutting tool for more delicate plants and flowers, without harming the roots. It also gives you the advantage of snipping just the plant you are trying to get at.

Utility Knife - This knife gives you the option of short or long blade use and safely retracts for convenient storage in your bag.

Pruning Snips - For sturdier stems or small branches, snips make collecting a breeze (e.g. Goldenrod).

Weeding Tool - This works perfectly for digging around tap roots like Dandelion or Thistle. A long bladed knife can be used, just take extra care when storing in your bag. Recommendation for this is to make a sheath for the blade. This can be as simple as using duct tape wrapped around a folded piece of heavy cardboard.

Gloves - Beneficial to protect you from plants that may be harmful to your skin. I prefer a good pair of rubber dishwashing gloves, as they are thick, strong and inexpensive. Great if you are collecting Stinging Nettle and they are usually a bright color, so if you lay them down in the grass, they are easy to spot quickly. Right you are, I've lost a few pairs. Hahaha!

Paper Bags - I carry various sizes, but find paper lunch bags are easy to attain and very affordable. Paper bags are breathable, this prevents plants from moulding. It is also a solution to easy separation when collecting a variety of plant species.

Reusable Shop Bag - Grocery style bags are perfect to have on hand to put all the smaller bags you have put separate plants into for easier transporting. It is also an excellent size bag for collecting larger quantities of a single species. If your bag has any kind of plastic lining, be sure to remove it immediately upon arriving back home. Otherwise plants shall mould and all your efforts shall be wasted.

Field Guide - An invaluable tool to guide you in all seasons. Since you shall be carrying it with you in your foraging bag, I suggest it be a smaller book, keeping larger plant reference books at home. Do not make my mistake and presume you shall just know the plant when you see it.

Notebook & Pencil - I keep a small ringed notebook in my bag to remind myself of places I've found specific things, information I might find useful or to sketch a plant I wish to research. This is also where I keep my foraging list and can tick it off as I find my plants. If I can't find everything on my list, it's still there the next time I go out. Having a pencil versus a pen, my pencil won't run out of lead or freeze up in the winter and I can sharpen it with the knife in my bag.

Other optional tools I carry in my car….

Chisel, Small Saw or Hatchet - These come in handy when you come across or are foraging tree barks, Chaga or any tougher plants and fungus. A convenient little saw that fits nicely into a foraging bag is a drywall saw or folding tree pruning saw.

Garbage Bags - These are not really to put plants in, although you could if you're that industrious. They are more to provide a base in your car to lay the plants upon and avoid a mess. The larger bag also gives a means to easily bundle and carry your natural treasures from the car into the house.

So now that you have your bag and tools organized, it's time to create your space.

You will need some various sized jars to keep your dried herbs in. Glass or ceramic is the best to store your plants in, plastic is an unhealthy choice whether in baggies, jars or containers. Plastic does not keep the integrity of the plants like glass can.

Some form of labeling system is required, this can be as simple or fancy as you wish it to be. There are many types of labels available or simple masking tape shall do too.

A place dedicated to your treasures once they have finished drying or cured. This can be a shelf, cupboard, pantry or even a tote. The main objective is very little to no light so the potency of the herb is not diminished.

What to do with your plants once you get them home. There are many options, drying, infusions, tinctures, salves or lotions. I personally prefer drying, after foraging for hours or all day, it's been wonderful but I'm running out of steam. It's better to clean and sort your plants right away, once they begin to wilt, they can become a tangled mess. Drying is the quickest and easiest process and once dry I can still make them into whatever I wish. Note, you can make tinctures, infusions, etc... from fresh plants too, but I find this more time consuming. I also try to plan my collecting quantity to fit my time schedule once I return, knowing I have to put them away.

To dry your plants, it's best to have a rack or some system in place for you to hang them up or lay them out. The placement of any rack should be in a dry, well ventilated area that has very little to no light. A spiritual energy tip, before you start to bundle your plants. Put as many positive thoughts into your heart and mind as you put your plants together, wrap the string around stems, hang them. Thoughts like how wonderful these plants will work or how healthy you, your family and household shall be. It's very surprising and fantastic, how much this boosts the positive vibration of your plants and always shows your gratitude for having been granted them, they are a gift…. not a right.

Start with your first species, grab no more than you can comfortably put your hand around with your thumb touching the tips of your fingers. Leave at least four inches of the stock or stem sticking above your hand. Have ready string or twine to tie around the bundle. I usually cut several pieces in advance, seven to eight inches long and separately lay them out on my work space table top. Then place the bundle end on the string, about three inches from the end of the stems. Tie once into a knot and wrap the rest of the string around stems, knotting a second time.

I have also made myself some elongated "S" shaped hooks from 20-gauge wire to loop one end under the tied string and the other end on the drying rack.

Now for a drying rack! There are many ways to go about this and the ceiling space is great for this. You'll require a bar of some sort, it doesn't even have to be straight.

Some suggestions are…. a sturdy branch, a dowel or curtain rod, a broom handle, as long as you can hang your bundles along it. Place two sturdy hooks (not cup hooks) into the ceiling about three inches shorter than your bar at either end. Wrap wire or string around the bar at the three-inch indent, make a loop at the other end and hang on hooks. Now you just hang your bundles using the "S" hooks, you can use just the string, I just find the hooks convenient for quicker removal. Let your plants dry naturally (away from sunlight).

This is just one way of making a rack, there are many ways…. Time to get creative!

BEGINNING TO FORAGE

It's been many, many years of playing with nature, roaming fields, forests and waterways. Hours of researching, studying and caring for all I've collected.

Looking back now, I've not regretted a single adventure. It's been one of the most self-satisfying of my achievements. This knowing that I can be completely self-reliant is astounding. This is a profound area of our nature that has become forgotten, a thing of the lost past. We've become completely dependent on commercialism for every aspect of our daily function, thoughts and entertainment. I find I'm just not satisfied with this way of life for myself and certainly not for the results it has on humanity nor our planet. It is my aspiration to rattle a few doors with this book. May they be thrown wide and knowledge be gleaned.

Let's start to forage!

First thing on your schedule is to decide what plants you are looking for. Whether it's to make medical and household products or edible plants for food, perhaps a little of both. Once you become more acquainted with a general variety of plants, you'll be able to just go on a curiosity hunt or with a shop list much like you do when going to the store. But for now, start with just choosing a few.

As much fun as it would be to just collect a mass amount of every kind of plant you find, and it shall be tempting. There is the little matter of the prep work and caring of your collection once you get back home. The sorting and drying should be done straight away for logical reasons. They are much easier to deal with while they are fresh (e.g... Tying, sizing or removing certain parts). If making tinctures, it's convenient to jar those plants right away if working with the fresh plant. The next step is to choose your location and check to make sure it's a chemically clean area. A few simple questions or calls will get your answers for you. People are usually quite reasonable, when you tell them you are foraging plants.

Okay, time to get your bag of supplies ready and check your list to make sure you have all you shall need. Add some seeds or nuts to the list, it's a very respectful routine to give Mother nature's children an offering.

It keeps the circle of abundance flowing, you receive.... you give back. That's a show of gratitude and the rewards of it shall flow back your way.

All right then! Time to get your hands dirty. You're off to the forest, meadow or backyard. Remember to be mindful when walking your path. There may be plants underfoot that you may not be collecting today, but may become important at a future time. Everything has a purpose and a life, care for them wisely with integrity. Once you find your plant, have a good look at the plant, checking for its state of health. You want a nice vibrant colored plant, without a lot of insect holes. The lighter the color, the younger the plant is. This makes for better taste most times if you are collecting for food and a higher potency if you are gathering for medicinal purposes.

Harvesting integrity plays a part here, you take enough for your needs, but also leave enough for regrowth and for our forest creatures too. This applies to how you harvest as well. When collecting flowers or leafy parts of a plant, it is best to use scissors to gently snip the plant an inch or two above the soil line. If you only wish the leaves, then snip these close to the stem. This leaves the flower and stem intact to reproduce the leaves and reseed. To harvest just the root of a plant, dig up the entire plant, cutting away the root and place the plant back into the hole you have dug. It may re root itself if wet enough soil or go to seed assuring regrowth. Take sparingly from one area to allow more to grow, unless we're talking about Dandelions which thankfully are never in shortage... And may they never be.

When harvesting tap roots, the best way to get them out is to push your weeding tool or long bladed knife straight down beside the plant about an inch away from the stem and do this all the way around the plant. Now take hold of the base of the stem, holding firmly and wiggling back and forth, while very gently pulling upward.

The absolutely best time to make it so much easier is early in the morning before the dew evaporates or just after a good rain. When it hasn't rained and you are in need of the tap root, you can take a jug of water with you to saturate the ground before you harvest it. Then follow the same steps as previously explained.

There are various ways to harvest many species and bark too. Once again, do your homework before you just blindly take it. The main objective is to be respectful of the environment and not harm the plants, shrubs or trees. There are also many video tutorials if you require a quick lesson (e.g. to properly remove bark from trees). Be kind to nature and your rewards shall be greater than you can imagine. Now that the fun has begun, why not enlist the aid of family or friends and make a day of it. It's a wonderful way to have an outing with the whole family, you and the kids, just you and your special partner or perhaps a girl's day out.

Take a thermos of whatever you like, a picnic lunch in a knapsack (leaves your hands free for foraging) and you have the makings of a spectacular day.

It's a win-win all around, fresh air, good company and you're getting paid in trade. Medical, household and food supplies, plus the raising of your own health with a higher vibrational mood and exercise. Best therapy ever!

When you go into nature with concerns or challenges, you come back with a new found sense of peace and calm. You may think this a bit far-fetched for some and you would be correct in your assumption. Not everyone is willing to pull the plug on their own personal dark thoughts.

Everything in nature is too much or not enough for some, too many bugs, no cell signal, the path is too uneven, etc....and so it goes. They cannot allow themselves the beauty to just be in the moment and therefore miss out on a wondrous opportunity to cleanse their spirit.

Of course, this is not you, or you wouldn't be reading this book :))

I have many fond memories of walking into the forest in one frame of mind to feel as if I had passed through a magical veil into another time and place. Even the air was different somehow and the symphony of birds chirping, the squirrels chattering, made all my heavy thoughts fade to a place of unconcern.

I would search and explore with Rascal stomping and romping about. It was different each time and every bit as magical as the first experience. One thing was very apparent, my thought process was not the same when I came out as when I went into the forest. My perception was much clearer and sharper, thereby making the issues laying heavily on my shoulders seem much lighter. I had a new insight at which to resolve those issues. Never underestimate the power of the trees, soil and the magic of the Earth.

Once you get a feel for spotting plants and you gain knowledge of the benefits to you and your household, a whole new world shall open to you. There is no limit to what you can create. The majority of people these days have no idea the depth to which we have been debilitated, mind, body and spirit. We have continuously been manipulated by the majority of people in authoritarian positions who say they have our best interests and safety in mind when they release statistics, regulations and laws. We trust with our hearts like children and allow ourselves to be led down the garden path to our misfortune. On many levels we are constantly deceived, misled and completely influenced by what we have been told. This has been done with such success, that when companies like the Pharmaceutical industry display advertisements and blatantly declare the horrendous side effects, we simply ignore it and swallow the medication regardless of the warning.

If the population read the ingredient list to these medications, vaccinations, food, household, body products and understood the detriment of those ingredients…. Everyone would be appalled!

Unfortunately, not only are we the lab rats, but so is every living being that is willing to be a party to this mass cruelty for large corporation's profit and control. My heart is deeply saddened for the ones that have no say in the matter, our children, animals and our planet. We don't have to be a society of cancerous, diseased, illness and unbalanced existence.

But it is a choice, to stand out and not follow the crowd, to think clearly for yourself in what is truly the very best for you and your family.

Even our clothes are designed to bring illness and discomfort to our health. It is very difficult or affordable to find or buy natural fiber clothing. Our textile industry produces clothing made with plastic fibers and many use inhumane labour from less fortunate countries. Please give this a thought when choosing your shopping location to make a purchase, example …. Dollar Stores. Let us also not forget our beloved fur family we think we are making good healthy choices for by taking them to the vet for vaccines that are as toxic to them as our human variety. The food created for our fur friends is also by no means considered food, no matter how expensive it is. Have you ever wondered why our domestic animals are being diagnosed with our human ailments or wild birds and animals who we feed also get sick or act strange, out of character? It's all the toxins, put in everything we come in contact with and consider normal. It's not an amazing leap!

We do not have to live like this. Our wonderful planet Earth has everything we require to live a disease and illness free life. Even with all the damage we've done to her, she still gives back. We have become a greedy society thinking only of our comforts, entertainments and as hypocrisy would have it…. It's killing us slowly.

All the elevation in technology is well and good, with our talking refrigerators, wristband cell phones, advanced tablets and phones…. No one is asking the important question. How is this affecting the human collective on a physical or mental capacity? Well, I'll give you a hint at the answer…. radioactive poisoning.

It has been happening gradually for decades and we have been oblivious to the side effects. As technology has advanced so has illnesses on many levels. Perhaps you are prone to headaches, ever find out why?

Headaches! Now there's a subject close to my life path. For years I've suffered with the pain of migraines, so I was told. That's actually how I got my push to complete natural living and was ridiculed for it as well, until it became a more popular practice in the collective.

The medications prescribed by my family doctor were making matters so much worse and running me into the poor house. One pill was approximately $20 dollars Canadian, thirty years ago that was a lot of money. Especially since it was only good to abort the headache, not cure it once you had it. I became a pharmaceutical guinea pig and worse yet, I became allergic to the sun from its side effects.

I was a single mother to four sons, my oldest being about seven at the time. It was extremely difficult to be hidden away from the sun and raise four young boys, look after farm animals and work too without any help, other than the boys pitching in.

I looked like one of those old vampire movies…. sunglasses and every inch of my skin covered. I had to wear hats with scarves around my neck, since my skin burned even under my hair. If I didn't do this, I really did take on the persona of a movie vampire. My skin would blister and bubble within minutes of the sun shining on my skin. It was not fun, then one day I was directed to a local health food store and my life turned upside down for the better.

Taking the salesperson's advice, I tried a remedy for my headaches. It cost me $11 for a three-month supply, at that price I thought, "why not try it". It was one of the best choices I made for my health. After my next month of being headache free, I gave up ALL my pharmaceutical medications as well as all over the counter products too. My quality of daily living escalated dramatically in a very short time.

There was a free library of natural healing books you could sign out at this health store and I made use of every opportunity I could to expand my knowledge. That was more than thirty years ago and this was my second leap of faith into a chemical free lifestyle. My research taught me that certain foods released chemicals in the brain that also contributed to increased pain. This was the opening door to eating wild plants and I've never been happier to cross a threshold. It began with learning that spinach absorbs calcium. I had plenty of aching muscles and joints, not a good resource I thought, so I switched the spinach with Plantain. It was so easy to go look for it, it was growing all over my lawn and down the driveway. I never sprayed any chemicals on my lawn, so therefore felt it was safe to pick. Soon I found my muscle aches lessened as well and my energy level increased. My next epiphany was about my cleaning products that I used around the house. I took notice of my headaches emerging when I cleaned my house and certain products were worse. Reading and researching came to my aid once again. I discovered several plants that possessed antibacterial agents in various levels of potency. To my pleasant surprise, I found a variety of these plants growing in a nearby ditch.

One of the best benefits that made itself known, was the increase in my financial savings. I found I could make a four liter supply for 95% less than the shelf price of regular cleaning products. Plus, the benefits just kept getting better!

Can you use your toilet bowl cleaner to wash your face or shrug your shoulders in carelessness if your child or animal friend happened to swallow some...? No you could not. But if you made your own from these plants it is perfectly safe, you could wash your face, your child or animals could swallow this substance safely, it just wouldn't taste very good.

My experiences and natural creative juices have just kept expanding over the years to where I began experimenting in making different products like scented waters for flavours and to make my own room deodorizers. Having essential oils are wonderful…. If you buy a quality brand, if your source of purchase can always get to you, and if you can continually afford them. It is convenient if you can't get out to forage the plant you need or the plant does not grow locally for you or it's the wrong season to collect and your supply has run out. However, foraging is my first choice as it only costs me an enjoyable walk and I know exactly what is in my recipe and every product you use in your household has a natural recipe.

It's up to you to create it or find it, but the rewards to your quality of life….

Priceless!!!

DEVELOPING DAILY ROUTINES

Daily routines can set the pace of your day and the productive way it functions. This is no different when organizing a natural lifestyle. As a good friend always reminds me, "It's making the unfamiliar, familiar" and this is not as hard as it may sound. The days are really the same, just different and better products are used in identical ways. It may seem overwhelming where to begin when first starting out so it is best to choose a few things you would like to replace or change to give you a better idea. An all-purpose cleaner is a great place to start, laundry detergent is another or there may be items on your list that could be causing problems.

One thing I constantly hear, "Well, I still have three or four bottles of cleaner, but as soon as they are empty, I'll switch over." How does that even make sense! You are first putting a limit on your road to good health. A bit like playing Russian Roulette....

Cancer doesn't care about time, it can decide to strike today, tomorrow or whenever it feels like, just like any other disease or illness. Do you truly wish to take that chance with yourself, your family or furry critters?

It really is a simple choice…. Do you want good health and clean living or you do not! How many people throw out products because it is a day past the marked expiration date, which is truly laughable, there is so much chemical preservative in our foods our internal organs are already rotting from the inside out…What's an extra day.

Everything that comes in contact inside or outside of your body is important, more than the money you think you are saving. It is always the smallest of things that escape our notice but may cause the most harm. Just think of how many things are invisible to us but can be deadly (e.g. Carbon monoxide). I was put in exactly such a circumstance when I lived at a farm in a secluded area. I rented this farm and was told the water system worked on a cistern. The water was safe for showers, toilet, laundry, but not to drink it from the tap. However, it was also deemed safe to use if I boil it for cooking purposes.

All was fine until I hit my second year of occupancy. I noticed my energy levels were fluctuating and continual stomach cramps. There was always a plausible reason for this at the time, or so I thought. I finally gave in and made an appointment with my naturopath to get some answers. Other than my symptoms, she said, I was in perfect health. Then she asked, "Have you tested the water?" I told her I didn't drink the water. "Do you cook with it?", she asked. "Well, yes," I replied, but I pre boil my water first. "Always?", she persisted.

This made me think deeper into my routine and I realized…. Not Always!

It brought to mind all the times I had rinsed my vegetables for salads, my herbs. Even eggs after hard boiling them were rinsed under the cold water from the tap. I had the water tested, and sure enough, it tested positive for E Coli. It took two years of my careless water habit to give myself E coli poisoning. I had asked and taken her advice, but refused her remedies, for I knew what had to be done and what plants would cure me. To my credit, by this time I had many years of research and experience accomplished and it certainly paid off. You just never know when this knowledge is necessary and you never stop learning. To this day my approach with any subject is to learn with an empty cup philosophy even when I may think it's the same brew. You can never be sure there is not a grain of extra knowledge to be acquired. The main lesson is to do what is right for you, regardless of any outside influences. All the money in the world cannot buy you quality of life when your body and mind fail you. The same can be said for your emotional and mental stability, if you allow comments or situations to influence your wellbeing and quality of living. Our quality of life does not come from a place, lectures or a book, it comes from within, a deep knowing that guides us. It is a saddening thought that our standards of what good health should be is manipulated by industry and social pressures. Once you have made a few changes and continue to add to this transitioning lifestyle, it's important to keep it going. I'm a list keeper myself, it helps me to stay on top of things. I had started with a list of products I had made on one side of the sheet and a list of products I wished to add. I also constructed a second sheet that was my "Plant Inventory List", this kept straight what plants I had and those yet to be collected or needed replacing. These sheets were kept taped to the inside of a kitchen cupboard door. Convenient and right where I needed them. I also left a space beside the "Products Made" list, to check off in pencil when I was running low. This kept me from running out as some products need to cure for weeks, so not always easy just make and use, the key is to stay ahead. As time went on, I had a shop list on my refrigerator door with two columns.

One was "Needs From Forest" and the other "Needs From Store". The store column became shorter and shorter as my skills elevated.

Spices and herbs were an easy switch, I just replaced one or two of the ones I had to organic each time I did a store shop and added my dried foraged plants with the rest. You would be amazed at the fillers that are used and put in the average spice bottle, and also the amounts of pesticides used to grow them. Another handy tip is labeling all my jars with the name on the front of the jar and a label on the back noting what the contents accomplish.

Also a warning written in red for any important notifications. I found for convenience at a glance, I use different colored pens to separate each benefit I use more frequently (e.g. red for warnings, blue for respiratory, green for antibacterial, etc...). When creating your own product or remedy, you may require more than one or two herbs. This system has made it easy just to scan the jars for the color matching my search.

The days I decide to make a product, I always make it in a large quantity. This also saves time, especially when some products need a lengthy curing time. The goal is to build up your stock so you have plenty now and shall also have enough supplies, at least in dried stock to accommodate you from season to season. It takes a while to transform all your everyday products over to a chemical free household, but if you keep at each item one by one, before you know it the chemical products are gone. An important routine to stick to, is no new chemical products just to make it easier. Any item you think you want to buy for convenience, has a natural substitute and it would be such a shame after all your effort to change. Here is an example of a product substitute, when removing sticky labels etc..., instead of buying a product like "Goo Gone", why not make your own. It's quite simple, you just need oil and a citric acid. Any oil shall do for this, such as corn or vegetable, there's no need to use an expensive oil. Then make an infusion with the oil and any citrus peels like grapefruit, lemon, lime, orange or mix all for a really nice smell and maybe add a whole clove or two. You have now made a natural "Goo Gone", without the harmful residue left behind. Making simple products like this shall amaze you at the savings to be had. I make about 96% of all my products and one day I'll make my own soap and shampoo too, but I have good friends that make them and do such a lovely job, so maybe not :))

This is yet another way to lessen the load by supporting someone you know and trust or by trading something you make for what they make. You shall also find this catchy, like minded always find one another. I think it's a Universal rule:))

The day shall come, quicker for some than others to transform your household. This shall depend on your motivation and intention. Let's say you are someone who has many ailments wishing to experiment with the goal of improving your health quality and you discover quick success. Then you would have the impetus to transition much quicker than someone who has a, "Let's give it a try" approach. As I've said before, this lifestyle takes conscious effort, but it does not need to be hard work.

It's just different than we are accustomed to. When you do reach the stage of effectively transposing all of your household products, it shall be a simple matter to keep it functioning smoothly.

We come back to building a new routine and your lists are the perfect place to start. I even keep a copy of my foraging "Shop List" on my cell phone, since it's usually with me for information and photos. It's a good idea to take photos of plants you don't recognise to research at a later date. The importance of your list is the time frame, you never know when you come upon a great find or the season it's best to harvest in. I stress again, not all products you make are instantaneous, some require two to eight weeks curing time. There are also the right times to collect certain plants before they lose their potency.

Late Spring and early Summer is usually the best time for most plants to be at their maximum potency, unless you are tapping trees, it's early Spring. The month best for you shall depend on your individual area, January and February slow Winter months are a great time to plan out your foraging schedule. Myself.... I try to have the majority of my wild plants harvested by the end of August or just as you notice the trees changing their color for Fall. Many do collect right up to October and it is a personal choice. However, I look at it this way.... the plants may still look fairly green and be alive, but the juices flowing through them are already fading out for a Winter's nap.

The goal is to create good, strong products and use less rather than something of weak quality. This is also my reason for keeping my foraging supplies in my car. I may be driving somewhere to spot one of the plants on my list in a good place. It takes less than a few minutes to pull over, hop out and scoop up what you need, to then be on your way again. The times you would like to make a full day of it, well those you plan but they don't always have to be that way, spontaneity works very well if you are prepared. Mother Nature looks after you if you are willing to meet her half way.

I find it curious indeed, that nine times out of ten, the plants you are in need of are right there around you. My oldest son is afflicted with Asthma and his backyard is teaming with Goldenrod, Mullein and Thistle, when he's not whipping them down, that is. Three very good plants to have when dealing with respiratory issues like asthma, colds, flu, pneumonia or any lung and chest symptoms. Unfortunately, most people just hack them down or spray them with toxic substances. Most people know Mullein is edible but did you know the flower tassels on the Goldenrod plant are also edible. The next time you are out in your yard, have a good look around and don't be so quick to dispense with the "Weeds", they may just be your saving grace.

I immensely dislike that word "Weeds" or rather the derogatory meaning the collective gives it. The dictionary characterizes it as a valueless, wild growing plant, any undesirable or troublesome plant.

Our ancestors had much more sense, at one time it was considered foolish to allow the grass to overpower the Dandelions. They knew the ultimate value of that weed! It produces food, medicinal remedies and is extremely hardy. As many people today know, since they are willing to spend a small fortune on weed killers or hire someone to come spray their lawns. Ironic don't you think, paying for the deterioration of our health and that of our families, animals (both domestic and wild) and our future generations to come.

Something I've noticed about many of the houses that spray their lawns, some family members in their household have forms of memory loss. Some mildly forgetful to more severe issues such as Alzheimer's or dementia. Animals that use the yard, cats or dogs contract cancer or some other human disease. Such a shame many can't see the connections.

When you do make those unexpected stops to forage on the side of the road, don't forget to bring in your scavenged treasures so they do not wilt in an airless, hot car. Plus, in case you may not have had your notebook on hand, make sure to jot your notes down as soon as possible while things are still fresh in your memory.

It's best if you have a space to keep your drying racks up or available all the time. That way when you bring plants in randomly, it's no big deal to prepare and hang them right away.

Don't be in such a rush with the drying stage, the plant must be completely dry before packing away. If there is any moisture, even just a bit left in the stem, flower, leaf or root, it shall mould when placed in the jar. You could be adding it to an existing jar with more of this herb in it and all your efforts shall be wasted for it shall ruin the entire batch in the jar. Give the leaves the crumble test and the stems and roots, the snap test. If all is ready, then proceed to the next step…. Storage.

I like to use a fairly large piece of parchment paper. I start by folding the paper in half to get a nice crisp seam down the center, then it's laid down flat again. This is so when I have my majority of the leaves scooped into the jar, I simply lift each side of the paper, give a little shake towards the crease in the center. Then lift the edge over the jar opening and let the last of it slide into the jar. Seal and label your jar, storing it in a place where no or next to no light can hit the jar, diminishing its potency. The storage area should also be cool to room temperature, for this too can reduce the quality of your herbs over a short period of time.

Another benefit to you and our planet is the reduction of landfill. Since you are using glass jars, refillable containers and not buying as many prepackaged products, there is less and less trash or waste. A big win-win all around!

Except to those producing more waste.

Speaking of trash, this is yet another way to be efficient. Save things like jars, spray bottles, shampoo bottles or the like. Instead of throwing these away and buying a new container, just clean the used and keep for your next natural product. Small containers (e.g. mascara tubes, lip balm tubes or jars, sinus spray bottles, deodorant tubes, etc...) are absolutely invaluable and very costly to purchase new. You may be saying, "I don't have the space to keep it." Here's a tip for extra storage: decorate a box or wooden box (crate), put containers inside and use them as a side table, ottoman or plant stand. Here's yet another way to challenge your creativity. When there were my four sons and myself in the household, I put an average sized garbage bag out to the curb every third week and a recycling bin (not quite full) every six to seven weeks. Now that my children are grown and out on their own, it's just me and my rats. I now put out a grocery sized bag of trash every four to five months and recycle next to never, there's usually nothing to go out. I have made it my mission to find a purpose for anything and everything I can. If I can't compost it or repurpose it, then and only then does it go to trash. Although I try to make a stand where I can to fight against extra or unnecessary packaging. But the truth of the matter is, until we stand up in greater numbers and refuse to purchase unnecessary items, it's an uphill climb, slow and steady!

That is why till we make it to that goal, I try to repurpose whenever I can.

How about you!

MY FAVORED
PLANTS & HERBS

There are numerous plants, trees, herbs and fungi that provide us with expansive benefits, many of these benefits the human race hasn't even discovered. However, I have a few that I consider my favorite go-to's. Before I expand on them, I would like to discuss expectations of taste. We have become a society of extreme flavours, craving sweet, salty, spicy, etc…

Wild plants have milder tastes of sweet, salty or spicy and some are quite bitter. In many situations this is the very circumstance that has led to poor health in our modern day palate. Our taste buds reject the ability to abide bitter tastes, which is especially essential to a properly functioning liver and other organs as well.

There are many ways to lessen these bitter flavours of some plants. Picking younger growth is the best way to achieve a better taste. Changing the cook water is another way to combat this issue. The water must be exchanged at least two or three times. This process is fairly simple. Bring the water to a gentle boil, toss the leaves into the water. Swish them about for a few seconds, strain and refill the pot with fresh water and repeat the process one or two more times.

Other methods are adding flavourings such as other herbs or spices, perhaps something sweet, like honey or maple syrup. Keep in mind some plants are just plain bitter and there's not much you can do to change it. A very large factor of this is mind set too, it's about retraining your taste buds and how you allow your mind to think about your food. Some people can't get past their own perception that they are eating "Weeds". It's all fine and dandy to let the rabbits munch on them but now they are on your dinner plate. Then there are those who see their lovely flowers in the garden and cannot differentiate them from the vegetable garden. This was the case when I once served Daylilies to a dinner guest, it was one of many vegetables on the table.

Some were common, carrots and such but some were flowers from the garden. My guest had seen Pansies in salads before so tried that but refused to have even a nibble of the steamed Daylily buds or stocks. Such a shame, but more for me :))

The Daylily is a fabulous plant. The entire plant, roots, shoots, leaves and flowers are edible. A very bland tasting plant that takes well to dressing it up with another flavor. It is also very high in vitamins and minerals. Maple trees are also full of surprises, everyone thinks maple syrup but that's just the beginning.

In late Spring as the tree is teeming with light yellow flower tassels, these can be dried and used as a sugar substitute (a very mild sweet).

The leaves at this time also make a wonderful addition to salads and can be used in other recipes, just get creative. The leaves create a great base to make spring rolls too. They can also be pickled to keep over the long Winter months. But we are not done yet, do you remember those little helicopter pods we would toss up in the air as kids just to watch them twirl to the ground. Well we were playing with our food and didn't know it, our ancestors as children would have known this. At the base of these helicopter keys are oval shaped pods and inside are pea-like seeds. These seeds are very much like sweet peas and can be cooked in the same manner. Once you are willing to open your mind to Mother Nature's grocery store, you'll have a new perspective on every plant, tree and shrub around you. The very best part is you shall be eating living foods of higher vibrations, it's a very special feeling.

Perhaps you are still skeptical about how much good it can really do for your body and mental state. Well let me tell you a little near death to life story. I have always had a very special relationship with animals from the time I was an infant, so in my adult years it was no surprise people would come across abandoned or injured animals and bring them to me for care. This one time I happened to be directed to a baby bunny that had been hit by a lawnmower and thought dead, unfortunately it was left to fend for itself.

It was brought to my attention by a friend's daughter the following morning, so it had been left where it lay all night and the sun was shining down upon the body mercilessly. I too thought the wee thing was dead, and proceeded to lift it to bury it. He was so small, he fit in my hand like the size of a baseball.

To my surprise it's front paw twitched. I immediately took it in and made it comfortable on a towel, then quickly grabbed an empty box and rushed outside for supplies. First I picked plain grass for bedding, then I took stock of what the bunny would have been eating in the yard.

I found the plants he (soon to be called Bugsy) would have chosen and picked from these plants the ones that had the highest nutrition and healing properties. I chose Wild Lettuce (for pain and nutrition), Plantain (for pain, antibiotic, antiseptic & anti-inflammatory) and a good source of iron to build Bugsy's blood, also Dandelion (for

healing of internal organs, cleansing the bloodstream &
regulating blood pressure from the trauma). Next I set
the box on its side on the floor, placing a thick amount of
grass in the box. My goal here was to ease Bugsy's mental
state and show freedom, not captivity or entrapment. This
was important otherwise he would have just given up and
chosen death. I had to make him choose life. Besides,
his back legs were not functional, so where was he going
to go?

After I had his new home set up I got some clean cloths
and a container of lukewarm water.

I very carefully slid my hand under the towel he was
laying on, lifting his body in my hand. Gently I began
to wipe his body down with the water and dropped drips
of water into his mouth in an effort to rehydrate him.
Bugsy was becoming a little more alert, so I carefully
patted him dry and set him in his temporary home.
Then I set a few leaves of the plants I'd selected for food
close to his mouth. I really didn't expect him to eat, I
knew he was still in shock so I did what I did when my
children were sick. I gathered my paperwork, sat on the
floor beside the box where he could see me and talked
to him in a soft voice…. like a Mom. We didn't discuss
his misadventure, instead I crooned to him of the day he
would be able to run and play, and see his real mother.
I told him I would love him forever but he had to do
his very best to get well, that his Mom was probably

worried sick about him. I slept on the floor that night too and late in the evening he nibbled on some plantain. He had the option to choose whatever he wanted but he chose the Plantain, exactly what I would have offered to him first. The next day he was sitting up but still could not move, his back legs seemed to be paralyzed. I put vinegar packs on his legs while cuddling him, this drew out swelling and also pain. Day by day I could see improvement, but still no walking, never mind hopping. After a week there were many changes, he was eating well, drinking on his own, could stumble around if not fully walk on his own. He still fell over a great deal and he had taken to sitting beside me as I worked, he had even trained himself to go to the bathroom in one spot so I allowed him free roam of the room he was in. I was in love, when I picked him up for snuggles he crawled into my hoodie and slept. I almost gave into the thought that I would adopt him if he didn't improve. Then I immediately reprimanded myself for thinking any debilitating thoughts about his progress.

It is so very important in all things to keep faith, trust and belief in an infinite capacity or all is lost, and this was a life or death situation…. No second chance!

There were others in the household that wanted to constantly feed him treats like carrots, cabbage, fruit and lettuce. They meant well, but I was adamant about him eating just wild foods and to this day I believe it's what saved him.

That was about a week in and after that his good health increased till he was with me for two weeks and I pronounced him well enough to go home to his Mom. All the while I was tending to Bugsy, I also sent messages to his Mother. I kept a watch on the backyard at night and noticed an adult rabbit coming just before dark.

I found a shrub that was close to the ground and hidden in the far corner of the yard. Here is where I dumped Bugsy's soiled bedding and I left a piece of carrot or apple that was laced with my scent.

Mother rabbit soon came every night and took her treat, but it was my treat...and heartbreak to place Bugsy there one night and watch from the window as she came for her son.

The moral of this story... Eating wild food and positive belief can save you!

I honestly believe if I had given in and let Bugsy have food from our grocery store, he would not have healed or maybe not even lived. Makes me take another hard look at what we call food and medicine. Our society continues to fall deeper and deeper into a diseased state, even our domestic animals are contracting our illnesses, I ask…. Why!

Here are some of my favourite plants and why….

Keep in mind there is much more information on these plants, but this shall get you started.

DANDELION (Taraxacum officinale) (Edible)

An amazing little flower that you probably already guessed is very hard to get rid of, Thank Goddess! There is not much it doesn't do, it is medicine, food and a yellow dye source. Dandelion also belongs to the Sunflower family and the seeds can travel up to five miles. That's for long distance wishes:)))

In the early 1800's it was almost a mandatory crop in the average household garden. Its nutritional values include minerals, magnesium, potassium, fiber, iron, calcium and is rich in vitamin A, C, K and B6.

It is a completely consumable plant from flower to roots. The roots have been used as a coffee substitute or mixed with chicory. As a tea, it has a delightfully nutty flavor when the root is roasted. Wine and an ingredient to make root beer is another of its usages.

The leaves used in salads should be picked when they are young and a light green to avoid harsh bitterness. It can also be made into salad dressings, vinegars, oil infusions, dips, stir frys, a side dish…. the possibilities are endless. It is a good idea to dry stems, roots and leaves for Winter storage and to use as an herb in other cooked dishes. The flower is better frozen, as when you dry the petals, they turn to seed. The seeds can also be ground for use. There are several ways to use the flowers in bread and cake recipes. The key in using the flower is not to overcook it, so in stir frys, toss them in last just before done. In soups and stews they shall take on the other flavors.

Medicinally it can be turned into tinctures, tonics, salves or poultices.

Medicinal Uses:
Antioxidant, Diuretic, Balances Hormones, Detoxifies Blood System & Internal Organs, High Blood Pressure, Liver Health, Weight Loss, Aids with Feminine Health and Manages Blood Sugars, Diabetes.

STINGING NETTLE (Urtica dioica) (Edible)

Many shy away from this plant due to its sting without realizing, this is part of its charm. If you suffer from arthritic pain, just by touching the afflicted area to the plant, causes brief pain for a moment only to take all the pain away. Goes along with Murphy's law, "It has to get worse before it gets better." Nutritionally it is very high in iron, contains magnesium, potassium, calcium, phosphorus, sodium, Vitamin A, C, K and several B's.

It is also composed of flavonoids, beta-carotene and all of the essential amino acids. For those watching calories, Nettles contain 37 calories per 100 grams. This is a wonderful plant to use as a spinach substitute, in salads, teas and the seeds can be sprouted. People who are iron deficient, can replace their iron supplement by incorporating Nettle into their daily consumption with tea or sprouts.

There was a time I took Iron supplements that cost me about $40 per month, now it's free thanks to its growing rampant in wet areas. I actually take it no later than 3 pm or I'm up very late, or should I say into the early morning hours. It is very energizing to the mind and the body. When harvesting Nettles, it's best to cut young plants, about twelve inches in height. To insure its regrowth and prosperity, cut with scissors approximately one to two inches above soil line.

Medicinal Uses:

Antioxidant, Anti-Inflammatory, Diuretic, Allergies/ Hay Fever, Diabetes (Lowers blood sugars), High Blood Pressure, Enlarged Prostate Treatment, Vasodilator (Heart issues), Anticoagulant (Reduces bleeding, especially if taken just before surgery & aids post-surgery too), Relieves & Heals Burns & Wounds, Aids with Liver Health (Protects damage from toxins, heavy metals & inflammation), Joint & Muscle Issues (such as gout).

PLANTAIN (Plantago major) (Edible)

A very potent plant that hides right beneath our feet :))

You just have to look down at your walkway, lawn or along the side of your driveway. It is as common and in sight as Dandelions and just as ignored. There was a time it was revered for its accomplishments and has been in use for more than four thousand years.

This little gem is packed with iron, copper, zinc, magnesium, potassium, calcium, Vitamin A, C & K. There are many in this family but the most common is Broadleaf Plantain (Plantago majar), Plantain Narrow Leaf (Plantago lanceolata) and Seaside Plantain (Plantago juncoides). The best way to use Plantain is in a tea, tincture, salve or poultice.

An onsite method to make use of a Plantain leaf if needed away from home, is to pick a leaf and chew it into a mulch, then spit into hand and apply where needed. The seeds are also a very beneficial part of the plant in cases of emergency. Young seeds can be a nutritional substitute if needed for survival food. Older seeds tend to be tough and fibrous, but shall do if necessary.

Plantain seeds can also be ground into a powder, which can be added to another source of flour to boost nutrition value or used on its own. However, it takes a very large quantity of seeds to produce a worthwhile amount of flour to be used on its own. It does make a very beneficial and nutritional boost to soups, stews, smoothies, it can literally be added to anything. Sprouting these wondrous seeds would also have many perks to overall good health.

Most know Plantain as a pain reliever for sore, aching muscles and joints but that's not even the tip of the iceberg. Plantain does very well as relief from the common cold, flu and excels at helping with a dry cough, due to its content of glycerin and pectin found in pharmacy cough syrups. This little plant is like an instant hospital dispensary at your disposal.

If you are planning to use Plantain for your culinary purposes, I have a few recommendations. The young leaves make for a great addition to any salad or as a spinach substitute. I substitute spinach anyway due to its calcium absorbing properties. Plantain is higher in iron than spinach and I don't need to concern myself with my bone health. If you have arthritis, osteoporosis, etc…, I highly recommend Plantain over spinach. To store, it can be frozen much like you would freeze spinach, it can also be dried. Once dried, I have the option of sprinkling it on or in my food dishes.

MEDICINAL USES:
Anti-Inflammatory, Antiviral, Antioxidant, Antiseptic, Antibiotic, Anti-microbial, Antispasmodic, Reduces High Blood Pressure, Boosts Immune System, Reduces

Inflammation in the Lungs, Respiratory Issues, Bronchitis, Aids in Heart Health, Cholesterol, Management of Chronic Liver Disease, Bladder Inflammation (Urinal Inflammation), Kidney Issues (Renal Disease), Gastro Intestinal Issues, Intestinal Worms, Digestive Health (Bloating, stomach issues), Skin Issues (Sunburns, burns, wounds, scrapes, bruises, psoriasis, eczema), Jaundice, Hemorrhoids, Diarrhea, Constipation, Diuretic, Rheumatism (Joints & muscle pain), Diabetes, Insect Bites, Bee Stings, Colds, Flu, Fevers, Peptic Ulcers, Bone Health, Eye Health, Autoimmune (Leaky gut syndrome), Dysentery, Heartburn and Oral Protection of Gums.

So did I lie…. Quite a miraculous little plant!

CEYLON CINNAMON (Cinnamomum verum) (Edible)

Now here is a spice that is taken for granted. This spice comes in two main types, Cassia and Ceylon. Cassia has moderate health benefits but is considered of lower quality and much cheaper, plus it is considered toxic if too much is consumed. It is the type sold on most grocery store shelves and originally comes from Southern China and is now grown in other parts of Asia, which is why it is known as Chinese cinnamon. The color is dark brown to reddish brown with thicker sticks and a rough texture.

Ceylon, known as the true cinnamon, is native to Sri Lanka, it is light brown in color and the tight layers of the sticks are soft.

Although this cinnamon is more expensive, it is cherished for cooking, quality and health benefits, without the toxins that are found in Cassia cinnamon.

Ceylon Cinnamon is a must in any kitchen for all its beneficial purposes.

As an antioxidant it has a higher status than Garlic or Oregano, shields the body from the collection and build-up of free radicals, so that the body may detoxify without undue stress. It contains Polyphenols, this alleviates the immune system and is especially good for inflammation of the liver. Heart attack and high blood pressure are decidedly reduced by Cinnamon. It can improve Insulin resistance (Blood glucose and lipid metabolism) as well as reduce Oxidative stress (Free radical build-up).

Cinnamon also combats bacterial infections (Respiratory issues, Flu and colds). When combined with Cloves it has the capability to combat and stop the growth of Listeria and Salmonella. It promotes good dental health as well as freshens bad breath. A warning about oral use, if you have any open mouth or gum sores, it shall definitely aid in its healing process but shall also sting.

When treating cancer, it can lower the risk due to its bacteria fighting properties. Cinnamon inhibits cancerous tumor growth by protecting DNA from damage and cell mutation.

Cinnamaldehyde, found in Cinnamon also promotes cell apoptosis (The self-destruction) of cancerous cells. This is particularly potent when treating colon cancer.

To use it for skin issues is simply amazing, it promotes healthy skin cells, creating a clean and clear complexion. It clears infections, rashes and irritations plus battles allergic reactions, swelling, redness and pain. A warning when using Cinnamon on the skin, always mix it with a carrier oil, never place on the skin full strength.

Cinnamon reduces symptoms that provoke asthma attacks. Adding a Cinnamon stick to tea, water or juice is a good preventative measure. In cases of diabetes, it improves sensitivity to insulin and lowers blood sugar levels. Metabolism also functions better due to Cinnamon. Alanine enzymes are blocked to dissuade absorption of glucose into the bloodstream.

Extra energy and weight loss can be achieved when adding Cinnamon to recipes by reducing or omitting the sugar called for originally. It prevents and cures Candida by protecting against fungal bacteria and inhibiting yeast growth (Use as a preventative measure). Cinnamon is a natural food preservative due to its antimicrobial properties, food remains edible for longer periods of time.

Parkinson's, Alzheimer's and memory loss plague our society today, but did you know Cinnamon stops the build-up of a protein called Tau, that is a high factor in Alzheimer's disease. Parkinson's disease is aided by improving motor function, normalizing neurotransmitter levels and protecting neurons with the daily intake of Cinnamon.

Medicinal Uses:
Anti-Inflammatory, Antioxidant, Antimicrobial, Antibacterial, Salmonella & Listeria (Parasitic bacteria), Aids Cellular Health, Cancer Treatment, High Blood

MARJORAM (Origanum marjorana) (Edible)

A Butterfly attracting plant, growing in Mediterranean regions that packs quite a punch. It belongs to the Mint family and has a history of being used to flavor beer before Hops were discovered. Another name for the Marjoram plant is "Joy Mountain". This plant has no known side effect, but there is a warning to those taking blood thinners (it stops blood from clotting).

A good means to lower blood sugar if you have diabetic issues. Marjoram's cleansing properties make it a wonderful antiseptic and antiviral, used both internally and externally to treat wounds. Helps to avoid conditions such as sepsis and guards against tetanus. It combats viruses like colds, flu, respiratory issues such as bronchitis, relieves nasal congestion, larynx and aids many lung issues (e.g. asthma).

This mighty plant also protects from measles, mumps and chickenpox. Marjoram is considered a highly valued antibacterial, fighting infections such as food poisoning, malaria and infections of the skin, urinary tract, digestive system, candida and typhoid. In digestion issues it stimulates digestive juices, aids intestinal issues and bowel movements. As a diuretic it increases urination to expel unwanted uric acid, excess water, sodium and various toxic substances. Increased urination helps to reduce fat and lowers blood pressure which also benefits weight loss. However, remember to stay hydrated to keep your kidneys clean.

In the role of antifungal, Marjoram supports skin health battling fungal infections. It is known to rid athlete's foot and fungal issues under toe and fingernails. Also it treats dysentery that develops from various pathogens, including the forming of fungal infections. For pain this herb makes an excellent anti-inflammatory, aiding sore muscles, tooth pain, headaches, menstrual cramps and works on inflammation internally and externally.

It is highly supported for cardiovascular health (e.g. stroke, heart attack & hemorrhage in the brain). Also it acts as a vasodilator, both relaxing and widening the blood vessels. Marjoram is favored for people with conditions like atherosclerosis, greatly recommended to include it in their daily dietary routine. This herb is also noted for stress relief, with its sedative properties, it calms mild anxiety and depression by soothing the nervous system.

All in all, Marjoram is an excellent dietary addition in any household.

Medicinal Uses: (No known Side Effects)
Blood Thinner, Diabetes, Antiseptic, Antiviral, Antifungal, Antibacterial, Anti-Inflammatory, Sepsis, Tetanus, Wound Treatment, Asthma, Respiratory, Flu, Colds, Bronchitis, Nasal Congestion, Larynx, Measles, Mumps, Chickenpox, Food Poisoning, Malaria, Skin Infections, Urinary Tract Issues, Digestive System, Candida,

THYME (Thymus vulgaris) (Edible)

Here is a plant that has been used in many ways, dating back before Roman times. It is best collected from June to August when gathering from the wild, if growing a domestic plant, it benefits from loose sandy soil and frequent pruning. Most people know Thyme for its use in culinary dishes, but it goes far beyond that. In days of old it was common to place Thyme in a sick room so it would dispel germs.

Thyme was also placed in with clothing or in bed ticking (an old time mattress) and mixed in with rushes on the floor so that insects were kept at bay.

Warts and calluses were removed by a salve made with Thyme, fat and sand. Nowadays we would not bother with the sand, using a pumice stone and replacing the animal fat with olive or coconut oil. They also used it to gargle for sore throats or to aid in mouth care for teeth and gums. Thyme makes a great mouthwash for bad breath as well, it is in fact one of the ingredients in "Listerine" or chest rub ointments, such as "Vicks". Its antibacterial properties make it a good choice when dealing with respiratory issues, even bronchitis.

This herb is also a very valuable aspect to combat skin issues like acne or inflammation. Stomach and intestinal bacteria such as viruses or diarrhea are alleviated and it is strong enough to kill intestinal worms, great for your animal companions. As an antispasmodic it treats and prevents epileptic seizures and for cardiovascular health it reduces stress by relaxing blood vessels, thereby lowering blood pressure.

Thyme is rich in Vitamins A, C, K, E, B- complex, B-6, Beta-Carotene and Folic Acid. It also contains Potassium, Magnesium, Manganese, Iron, Calcium and Selenium. These minerals are at their peak potency when the leaves are young. Thanks to this rich source of vitamins and minerals, is it any wonder it's known to boost the immune system and also stimulate white blood cell formation, increasing the body's resilience against bacteria and viruses. If you are plagued with mood swings, depression or mental clarity issues, Thyme shall aid in reducing your stress, wonderful in an aromatic bath.

Medicinal Uses:
Antiseptic, Antiviral, Anti- inflammatory, Antispasmodic, Antiparasitic, Anti-fungal, Antioxidant, Anti-bacterial, Relieves Stress (Balances mood swings), Stimulates Blood Flow & Red Blood Cells, Circulation (Oxygenative), Heart Health, Respiratory Issues, Asthma, Bronchitis, Coughs, Mental Clarity, Dental Cavities, Gum Disease, Bad Breath, (Mouthwash), Sore Throats, Stomach Flu, Digestive Upsets, Diarrhea, Worms, Intestinal Issues,

GOLDENROD (Solidago canadensis) (Edible)

Many shun this forsaken plant and yet it continues to thrive and spread, against our unwise efforts to eradicate it. Goldenrod was also known at one time as Mountain Tea. We have called this plant a weed, falsely blamed it for causing allergies, when in fact it is the remedy for runny noses, clogged sinuses and so, so much more.

The antioxidant components rate higher in Goldenrod than in Green Tea and aids in fighting bacteria, making it a good choice as a body cleanse or even an ingredient in your cleaning products.

Antiseptic and antimicrobial properties make this a good choice for sore throats and as an expectorant, as it expels mucus easily from the lungs. The diaphoretic attributes of Goldenrod help open pores of the skin to release sweat during a fever. Also it's astringent properties calms runny eyes, noses and sneezing. Goldenrod contains Quercetin and Rutin which are natural antihistamines.

A warm tea can be made for a gargle to treat laryngitis and pharyngitis (sore throat). As well it drys bronchial and respiratory secretions and expels existing mucus.

The cardiovascular system also benefits from the source of constituent Rutin, a powerful flavonoid.

Rutin reinforces circulation for the cardiovascular system and increases capillary strength. Goldenrod boosts and improves the cerebrovascular system as well.

As an anti-inflammatory it reduces pain and swelling in turn relieving stress from gout, arthritis and other joint pain. It is very helpful towards ridding the body of kidney stones by acting as a prevention of them forming in the first place but also breaks apart existing kidney stones, thereby creating balance to the kidney's overall function.

The antiseptic properties in Goldenrod serve as a good treatment for urinary tract and bladder infections. It is also an antifungal, containing Saponins which make it useful for candida type yeast infections, boils or as a gargle for oral thrush. For skin issues the flower and leaves can be infused in olive or coconut oil to make a poultice for wounds, rashes, cuts, burns and open sores. It works well as a rub for aching and tired muscles.

Medicinal Uses:
Anti-inflammatory, Antiseptic, Antioxidant, Antihistamine, Antimicrobial, Antifungal, Diuretic, Bladder, Urinary Tract, Hemorrhoids, Irritable Bowel Syndrome, Allergies, Colds/Flu, Viruses, Digestive, Respiratory, Bad Breath, Gum Disease, Expectorant, Sore Throats, Candida, Vaginal Douche, Skin Issues, Eczema, Astringent and Cardiovascular.

THISTLE (Silybum marianum) (Edible)

Now most everyone knows what a Thistle is! We have at one time or another found ourselves traipsing around on the grass in bare feet, only to step on one. Ouch!

Of course that's not a good reason to exterminate the species when it bestows such advantages to not only us but animals and feathered friends alike.

Thistle is a member of the Aster/Daisy family (Asteraceae), it's flowers produce seeds that many birds love, especially the Yellow Finches.

This plant has many functions to aid in good health and nutrition. It strengthens the immune system, making it a natural antioxidant. The stomach reaps many rewards, for it stimulates the growth of beneficial bacteria in the gut and reduces the level of pathogenic bacteria. Aid is given to digestion issues like stomach cramps, bloating and also cleanses the colon, bringing relief to constipation. Heartburn is also given assistance by this plant.

Thistle works very well with Kidney function, lessening chances of developing Kidney stones. As an oxidant it aids Liver function, protecting the body tissue against damage from free radicals caused from the environment, poor dietary choices and chemical intake. A key component in Thistle is Silymarin, thanks to this substance, it contributes to aiding in weight loss. Lowering bad cholesterol (LLD) works with diabetes by lowering blood sugar levels and also reducing the body's resistance to insulin.

Anti-inflammatory properties in Thistle relieves joint pain and promotes calcium absorption. A tea or tincture made from the flowers or leaves is the way to go and they can be dried for future use, as well as made into a salve or lotion. Aches and pains are not the only inflammation that plagues the body, it is a solution for inflammation of the air tubes in the lungs so is a great treatment for Asthma and other internal organs. It also reduces inflammation of the skin, protecting skin tissue from damage during aging. Ladies, here is the plant for you if looking for a great ingredient for a natural wrinkle cream.

Jaundice inflictions and gallbladder issues is yet another area it brings relief to. Thistle is now being researched for its use in aiding hepatitis and Alzheimer's.

It has been found that oxidative stress is a high factor in causing Alzheimer's and it is believed that Thistle reduces oxidative stress considerably. Thistle leaves have estrogen tendencies that can stimulate blood flow and aid in the increase of milk flow when breastfeeding.

Thistle contains Vitamin A, C, E, B1 (Thiamin), B2 (Riboflavin), Potassium, Iron, Sodium, Magnesium,

Manganese, Zinc, Selenium, Copper, Calcium, Folic Acid, Niacin, Proteins and is a good source of Fiber.

The root also has a beneficial purpose, in aiding with healing skin rashes and relieving itching. Great for poison ivy, poison oak or insect bites. A good ingredient to use when making deodorant, as it reduces sweating.

Thistle is completely edible.... flowers can be steamed or par-boiled until tender, roots can be boiled, roasted, fried or even eaten raw. The outer skin of the stalks needs to be scraped or peeled, then can be cooked same as you would with the roots. For larger or thicker stalks, you may wish to soak them overnight to reduce any bitterness. The leaves can be dried for tea and future supply, used as a spinach-like substitute or in salads. To prepare leaves, use scissors to trim away the tynes.

When harvesting Thistle flowers, please remember to leave a sufficient amount for the birds and forest animals. The flowers supply much needed nutrition to them as well.

Another way to get Thistle into your system is to dry any part of the plant and grind seeds, crumble dried leaves to use in foods you prepare or grind very fine to use as a flour substitute.

Medicinal Uses:

Antioxidant, Anti-inflammatory, Antispasmodic, Hypoglycemic, Leaky Gut Syndrome, Stomach Cramps, Bloating, Constipation, Colon Cleanse, Diuretic, Kidney Function, Heartburn, Liver Function, Lowers Cholesterol, Weight Loss, Respiratory, Bronchitis, Asthma, Skin Issues, Rashes, Anti-aging, Relieves Itching, Jaundice, Reduces Sweating, Gallbladder Issues, Alzheimer's, Hepatitis and is a remedy for Mushroom poisoning.

SELF-HEAL (Prunella vulgaris) (Edible)

A lovely little flower that is highly taken for granted by most. It greatly serves our table and our medicine cabinet. This stalwart warrior plant has staunchly built up its barriers against its adversaries. Even the chemicals humans have thrown at it have not taken it down, says a great deal about its subtle strength.

Self-heal is a member of the mint family and grows just about everywhere. The young stems and leaves are favoured in salads, on sandwiches or as a topping on other vegetables. In medical affairs it has a long list of achievements. The Kidneys are strengthened and heat is removed from them. Due to its diuretic function, decreasing the surplus of body fluids thereby lowering blood pressure. Digestive issues are also aided, such as colic in infants, crohn's disease, heals ulcers, stops bleeding, soothes bloating and intestinal tissues. It is known to fight bacteria, fungal and viral infections including HIV and stops it from spreading.

Self-heal reduces insulin sensitivity regarding diabetes, as well it aids to normalize blood sugar levels and acts as a prevention to other related conditions like atherosclerosis. The anti-viral properties in Self-heal prevent virus outbreaks in the body (e.g. cold sores and genital herpes), also an aid for hemorrhoids. Self-heal has a cooling effect on skin issues such as wounds, burns, rashes, mouth ulcers, boils, eczema, insect bites or stings. It reduces and eliminates redness and swelling both internally and externally.

Treatment for the heart is also one of its claims, it reduces high blood pressure, making it a wonderful regenerative tonic for cardiovascular tissues and a way of preventing hardening of the arteries. This plant works to improve and detox Liver function, treats jaundice, hepatitis and strengthens the Liver. It is used to stop bleeding, inclusive of extreme menstrual bleeding. The immune system greatly benefits from regular use of Self-heal, combating infections, allergies, chronic inflammation, reduces swollen glands and clears toxins from the body.

Self-heal is also reputed to aid in stopping or slowing the growth of cancerous tumors and killing cancer cells.

Warning: To those taking blood thinners.... monitor your use of Self-heal. Discontinue use if side effects occur (e.g. skin rashes, dizziness, constipation, nausea, itching, vomiting or weakness).

Medicinal Uses:
Anti-inflammatory, Antioxidant, Antiviral, Antibacterial, Antifungal, Wounds, Cold Sores, Genital Herpes, Diabetes, Cancer, Liver Issues, Heart Issues, Viral Infections, HIV, Respiratory Infections, Allergies, Chronic Inflammation, Skin Infections, Insect Bites/Stings, Rashes, Itch Relief, Boosts Immune System, Kidney Issues, Lowers Blood Pressure, Ulcers, Digestive Issues, Crohn's Disease, Ulcerative Colitis (Irritable Bowel Syndrome), Hemorrhoids, Colic,

HIBISCUS (Hibiscus sabdariffa) (Edible)

A lovely flower that graces many a garden with its beauty, but beneath the glamorous appearance lurks a powerhouse marvel. This is an edible plant, its leaves, flower and seeds can be consumed. The calyx however, is what is most often sought after. Hibiscus sabdariffa is the variety mostly used for food, also known as Red Sorrel. A little fun fact you may not have known is that Hibiscus has many accompanying plant strands within itself, like Cotton, Okra and Cacao.

Hibiscus is no slouch when it comes to nutrition either, it is rich in Vitamin C, is a good source of fiber and contains Calcium, Phosphorus, Iron, Niacin, Riboflavin and Flavonoids. It has a lengthy list of medicinal benefits as well, such as reducing fat build-up in the Liver, which also makes Hibiscus a great choice in weight management.

For thyroid issues, drinking a cup of tea or applying a smooth paste to the scalp is very helpful. Ladies this is a little gem you might wish to add to your face and body creams or lotions list as it has anti-aging components. Want proof, take a look at the skin of the elderly on the islands. Hawaiians use Hibiscus in many things, food and products. They spend their days under the sun, on the salty beach and have vibrant, healthy skin. It is due to all the essential oxidants present in Hibiscus.

This plant has a cooling effect so is good to use when fighting a fever or pursuing relief from hot flashes during menopause. It calms the nervous system, thereby aiding in mood swings, depression and relieving symptoms from menstrual issues such as over-eating or cramping pain. Hibiscus brings benefits to heart health through a compound called Anthocyanin.

It naturally regulates blood pressure without altering levels of potassium in the blood or adjusting the balance in salt-water.

The leaves contain Polyphenol which gives Hibiscus anti-inflammatory properties. Hibiscus not only is beautiful but seems to be a beauty shop all on its own. Not only does it work well with our skin but does much for our hair as well, using it as a hair tonic can dissuade hair loss, slow the aging process of hair turning grey. It is actually one of the ingredients in red hair dye. There are several ways this plant can be utilized with a bit of creativity.

Medicinal Uses:
Antioxidant,Respiratory Issues (colds/flu, coughs), Anti-inflammatory, Anti-aging, Anti-cancer (especially Colorectal cancer), Boosts Immune System, Skin Wounds, Acne, Liver Health, Calms Nervous System, Thyroid Issues, Heart Health, Aids Blood Circulation, Varicose Veins, Lowers Blood Pressure, Stimulates Blood Flow, Hypertension, Lowers Cholesterol, Weight Management, Diabetes, Lowers

Blood Sugar Levels, Depression, Gastrointestinal System Health, Constipation (laxative properties), Menstrual Issues, Menopause (calms hot flashes), Prevents Hair Loss, Reduces Grey Hair, Repels Head Lice.

Warning: Peanut Alert! Due to compatible growing practices by large companies that grow Hibiscus for marketing. Hibiscus is sometimes grown side by side with peanut plants, this causes cross contamination.

Do Not Take If....

- You have Low Blood Pressure (may decrease even further).
- Taking Birth Control pills.
- You are on any Fertility or Hormonal treatments.
- Pregnant or a Breastfeeding mother.

Due to other plant strands in Hibiscus, use in small doses till you are certain it causes no ill effects for whomever is taking it.

Fertility drug levels of estrogen in the body are reduced, menstruation can be stimulated resulting in possible miscarriage.

NATURAL RECIPES

Tinctures and Oil Infusions have to be my all-time favourite way to store my herbs. It's quick, easy and takes minimal supplies to accomplish the end result, also it can be done with fresh or dried herbs.

Here I shall describe your basic method to make tinctures and oil infusions for the beginner.

TINCTURES

This is a way of extracting all the beneficial components from your chosen herb or plant into a liquid form that is absorbed into the body at a much quicker rate.

Tinctures are usually made with an 80 proof or 40% alcohol liquid such as Vodka or Brandy, any consumable alcohol will do, however using one with a lower sugar content is better. Vinegars or Glycerin base products can be used but have a lower shelf life of approximately two years, whereas alcohol's shelf life is indefinite.

Just make sure your jar is airtight to avoid evaporation.

Storage or curing time can be six to eight weeks, the longer it cures, the higher the potency.

*Choose a jar that will hold the amount of tincture you wish to make.
*Fill the jar ¾ way full of your chosen herb if using fresh and ½ way full if using dry.
*Pour Alcohol in the jar, over your herbs to within a half inch of the rim.
*Seal the jar, label and date.
*Give a good shake and store in a cool, dry place.
*Shake tincture once a day to help release the herbs benefits into the alcohol.

OIL INFUSION
There are two methods to make infusions, warm or room temperature.

The difference is the amount of time it takes to cure your oil.

One of the benefits of having your plants infused into an oil is that it is ready to use or made into a salve and provided it is sealed well once the curing is done it shall last about two years. Once again it is important to research the carrier oil you plan to use, making sure it is of good organic quality. Olive oil is the usual go to carrier oil but there is a large variety that can be used.

Also it is recommended to use dried herbs when infusing oil so as not to have moisture contaminate your oil with mold or turning it rancid. It is possible to use fresh but should be covered with cheesecloth and elastic, and watched closely.

Room Temperature Method -
*Choose the size of jar you wish to make your infusion.
*Fill the jar ½ to ⅔ with your chosen dried herb or plant.
*Pour your choice of carrier oil over herbs or plants leaving ½ inch headspace.
*Stir well, removing any air bubbles.
*Seal jar, label and date.

*Store in a sunny or warm spot for 6 to 8 weeks (a water bath of warm water can be done for several hours to give the oil a head start before resting the 6 to 8 weeks)

*After the curing period is finished, strain out herbs using cheesecloth to be able to squeeze all the goodness from the herbs (Leave herbs in oil no longer than 8 weeks to avoid spoiling).

*Do not boil your oil as it changes the chemical composite of the plant's properties.

Warming Method -

*Choose the size of jar you wish to make your infusion.

*Fill jar ½ to ⅔ with your chosen herb or plant.

*Pour your choice of carrier oil over herbs or plants leaving ½ inch headspace.

*Stir well, removing any air bubbles.

*Seal jar if using dried herbs, but leave lid off if using fresh herbs (I cover with cheesecloth and elastic). This allows moisture to evaporate out of the jar, be sure no water gets in from the water bath.

*Place in a crock pot, cooking on low setting for about 5 days.

*Make sure to keep an eye on your water level, that it is always topped up.

*Once oil is finished, let cool.

*Then strain with cheesecloth, squeezing into another clean jar.

*Label and date.

HERB COMBINATIONS

Here are a few combinations that I have used for various issues.

Please be sure to first check with your physician, naturopath or medical care giver, if pregnant or breastfeeding and if taking other medications, before attempting any of these home remedies.

Scented Waters -

*1 cup   Chosen Plant, Flower, Bark, Stock or Root

*¼ cup   Alcohol

*1 L.   Jar with tight fitting lid

-Place plant matter in the jar with alcohol.

-Boil enough water to fill jar, let cool a few minutes.

-Pour water into the jar allowing a half inch head space.

-Seal the jar and label it with the date.

-Give a good shake.

-Let sit in a sunny spot for 6 to 8 weeks.

-Shake every few days till cure time has elapsed.

This product can be used for many purposes, such as mixed with floor wash water, homemade cleaners and other products that require diluting.

Get creative!

Some examples are…. Pine Needles, Rose Petals, Citrus Peels, Hibiscus, Rosemary, Thyme, Peppermint, Lavender, Lilac, etc…. And the list is endless!

One of my personal all-time favorites is…. Lavender, Cloves and Lemon or Pomelo rinds.

When you create infused scents this way, it saves you a great deal of money.

However, the tradeoff is space, an essential oil bottle takes up less storage space on your shelf.
I also like to make these scented waters in individual scents, rather than mixed. This way I can make any combination at any time I wish, without having to wait for curing times.

Have fun and enjoy!

Mouthwash -

¼ cup	Thyme	*1 stick	Ceylon Cinnamon
1 tsp	Rosemary	*1 tsp	Goldenrod
1 tsp	Sage	*¼ cup	Parsley
¼ cup	Brandy	*3 ¾ cups	Water

Yields: 1 liter

-Bring water to a boil.
-Then set aside for a few minutes, allowing to cool slightly.
-Add all herbs and let sit overnight on the kitchen counter.
-Next day, strain liquid into a jar or bottle.
-Mix Brandy into the solution, cap and give a slight shake.

To Use: Gargle with about half an ounce when needed.

Toothpaste -

*½ cup	Coconut Oil	*1 tsp	Ceylon Cinnamon (Grd.)
*1 tsp	Thyme (Grd.)	*½ tsp	Marjoram (Grd.)
*½ tsp	Plantain (Grd.)	*1 tsp	Baking Soda
*⅛ tsp	Cream Of Tartar		

-Mix all ingredients together in a small bowl.

-Scrape into a jar, seal and label.

-Best if you can let sit for a week or more.

**If paste is too thick, add a bit more Coconut Oil

-You can also add extra flavours by mixing in a few drops of essential oil

(eg. Peppermint, Wintergreen or Lemon)

-When using Essential Oils, be sure to source your product well.

-Many have false claims of purity and combine synthetics with perhaps one drop of the pure oil. -This does not make it healthy for consumption.

Teething & Gum Gel - (Instant pain relief)

*1 tsp	Cattail Gel	*½ tsp	Ceylon Cinnamon (Grd.)
*¼ cup	Coconut Oil	*125 ml.	Mason Jar
*⅛ tsp	Cloves (Grd.)		

-Mix all ingredients in a small bowl.

-Scrape into jar, seal and label.

-Let sit for approximately 1 week.

**For emergencies use Cattail Gel directly on the affected area, Use Sparingly!

(Best time to collect Cattail Gel is in late Spring)

This remedy can also be used on Animals, to help relieve pain for our fur family.

Eye Wash -

*1 tsp	Chamomile	*1 Tbsp	Colloidal Silver
*1 tsp	Eyebright	*¼ cup	Distilled Water
*1 tsp	Plantain	*250 ml.	Mason Jar

-Bring water to a boil, let cool for a few minutes.

-Place herbs in a cup.

-Pour water over herbs and let sit for 3 to 4 hours (Unrefrigerated).

-After sit time is complete, strain liquid into the jar.

-Stir in Colloidal Silver.

-Seal, label and date.

-Keep refrigerated, shelf life approximately 4 to 6 weeks.

**To avoid waste, it can be made in smaller quantities.

Uses: Tired, itchy or sore eyes. Pink Eye, Styes and Infections or swelling.

Face & Body Cream -

*¾ cups	Coconut Oil	*1 Tbsp	Ceylon Cinnamon
*1 Tbsp	Olive Oil	*1 Tbsp	Shaved Beeswax (optional)
*1 Tbsp	Hibiscus Petals (crushed)	*250 ml	Wide Mouth Mason Jar
*1 Tbsp	Thistle Seed (Grd.)		

-Warm oils and stir in Hibiscus Petals, Ground Thistle Seeds and Ceylon Cinnamon for about 1 hour.

(This can be done a few different ways….
  1. By placing oils and ingredients in a double boiler.
  2. By placing the jar filled with oils and ingredients in heating water in a pot or a slow cooker.

-If not already in a jar, pour warmed oil and herbs into the jar now.
-Label and date.
-Let this solution rest for 6 to 8 weeks in a cupboard.
-Once solution has cured, warm again till oil is in liquid form.
-Strain oil from herbs, pouring it into a clean jar and label.
-If a firmer consistency is desired, keep warming the strained oil and add the beeswax, stirring constantly.

-Then pour quickly into the jar, scraping the warming pot.
-Place in the refrigerator for an hour to solidify.

**To avoid clogging your drains from the wax residue, wipe your pots and utensils with a paper towel or newspaper immediately after your warming is complete.

Acne & Blemish Cream -

*¾ cups	Coconut Oil	*1 tsp	Hibiscus Petals (crushed)
*2 Tbsp	Olive Oil	*1 tsp	Marjoram
*1 tsp	Thyme	*1 tsp	Ceylon Cinnamon
*½ tsp	Ground Charcoal (optional)		

-Warm oils together with herbs for about 1 hour.
-Pour into a jar, seal, label, date and let rest for 6 to 8 weeks in a cupboard.
-Once cured, warm again and strain, pouring oil into a clean jar.

For a stronger night version of this cream, a small amount of cream (2 Tbsp.) can be mixed with charcoal (½ tsp) and used at bed time. Then washed off in the morning.

This cream can also be used as a face cream to retard acne, blemishes and skin issues from forming.

For existing skin issues, I recommend adding ½ tsp each of ground Red Rose Petals and Rosehip (very good for Rosacea).

Chest Rub -

*1 Tbsp	Olive Oil	*1 tsp	Cedar Leaves (crushed)
*¾ cups	Coconut Oil	*1 tsp	Oregano
*1 Tbsp	Thyme	*1 Tbsp	Rosemary

-Warm oils with herbs for an hour.

-Pour into a clean jar, label and date.

-Let rest in a cupboard for 6 to 8 weeks.

-Once cured, warm again and strain oil into a clean jar.

-Label and date (shelf life about 4 to 6 weeks)

To Use: Rub on chest or under nose when congested. Also good for headaches, rub on temples.

All Purpose Cleaner -

I make my cleaners in a 4 Liter quantity so I have plenty on hand and restart my next container when it's about half empty. This way I never run out.

Basic Recipe....

*3 ½ L   Clean Water or Scented Water (Your choice from what you've made)
Or 30 drops of Essential Oil added to water.

*½ cup   Natural Soap Flakes or 8 Soap Berries
(I buy Nature Clean Dish soap and sometimes use this in place of the Natural soap flakes)

*4 L   Container, Jar or Jug.

-Pour water in a container (Do this first, before adding soap.... otherwise you'll have a sudsy overflow).
-Add soap and cap.
-Gently turn the container upside down, then upright to mix water and soap.
-Do not shake!
-This is now a concentrated solution.

To Use: Pour your required amount for your purpose into a bucket or where needed, then add extra water, vinegar or lemon juice.

Furniture Polish -

*½ cup	Pine Needles	*½ cup	Lemon or Orange Peels (Or Both)
*¾ cups	Canola Oil	*500 ml.	Mason Jar

-Place Pine needles and Lemon/Orange peels in the mason jar.

-Pour the oil over the needles and peels, leaving a half inch head space.

-Seal the jar, label and date it.

-Shake vigorously, till all within is coated well.

-Let sit in a cupboard for 6 to 8 weeks.

-Shake every few days to release scent and natural oils from needles and peels.

-After cure time has passed, strain oil into a clean jar or bottle.

To Use: pour some onto a soft cloth and rub into your wooden piece.

Grease Scrub -

*½ cup	Epsom Salt	*2 tsp	Ceylon Cinnamon
*½ cup	Baking Soda	*2 Tbsp	Bladder Campion (Powdered)
*¼ cup	Cream of Tartar		

-Mix all ingredients together in a container.
-Scoop out and use the same as soap with water.
-Scrub and rinse your hands with hot water.

Ulcer Tonic -

*1 cup	Plantain Leaves	*½ cup	Raw Honey
*¼ cup	Poppy Seeds	*1 cup	Self Heal
*½ cup	Organic Lemon Juice or	*2 L	Water
*2	Organic Lemons		

-Bring water to a boil, then reduce to low heat.

-Add Plantain leaves, Self Heal and Poppy seeds.

-Let simmer on low heat for 10 minutes.

-Strain into a jar, adding honey and lemon juice.

-Stir till Honey is dissolved.

-Drink warm or at room temperature.

-Keep refrigerated.

Dosage: ¼ cup per day till symptoms disappear.

**It is very important to use organic Lemon juice or Lemons, due to harsh pesticides used on non-organically grown.

Energy Snack -

*1 cup	Coconut Oil	*2 Tbsp	Nettle
*½ cup	Raw Honey	*1 Tbsp	Ceylon Cinnamon (Grd.)
*2 Tbsp	Sesame Seeds	*1 Tbsp	Dandelion Root (Grd.)
*2 Tbsp	Hemp Seeds	*2 Tbsp	Marjoram
*¼ cup	Walnuts (Grd.)	*1 Tbsp	Cardamom
*¼ cup	Pecans (Grd.)		

Optional Extras: Chopped Dried Fruit, Other Seeds, Shredded Coconut,
Peppermint Leaves, Shaved Dark Chocolate, Other Nuts, Dark Cocoa Powder, etc.…

-In a small to medium size bowl stir coconut oil and honey until smooth and creamy.
-Add all other ingredients and mix quickly.
-Check taste to see if it suits yours.
-Scrape into a 8x8 glass baking dish, smoothing it out to the sides.
-Put it into the freezer for 30 minutes.
-Remove from the freezer and score into desired size squares or bars.
-Put back into the freezer till solid.
-Then remove from the baking dish to an airtight container and return to the freezer.

These snacks pack a powerful shot of filling energy.

Great way to start the day.

They do however need to be eaten relatively quickly and do not travel well.

You can also toss one in a smoothie for extra nutrition.

Thank-you for joining me on my first public writing challenge.

I have thoroughly enjoyed sharing my experiences and knowledge with you, may you also find rewarding benefits on your new found journeys.

It is my greatest wish to see humanity awaken to the natural treasures Mother Earth holds for each one of us, if we but accept her bounty gratefully.

Brightest of Blessings to you all!

Erika
(AKA The Red Witch)
Red Witch Studios

Printed in the United States
by Baker & Taylor Publisher Services